Addiction

Addiction

How Christians Can Respond Positively to a Growing Crisis

Walter E. Kloss

REVIEW AND HERALD PUBLISHING ASSOCIATION
Washington, DC 20039-0555
Hagerstown, MD 21740

The author assumes full responsibility for the accuracy of all facts and quotations cited in this book.

This book was
Edited by Richard W. Coffen
Designed by Richard Steadham
Cover photo by Meylan Thoresen
Type set: 11/12 Melior

PRINTED IN U.S.A.

Library of Congress Cataloging in Publication Data

Kloss, Walter E., 1927-
    Addiction.

    Includes bibliographies.
    1. Drug abuse—United States.   2. Drug abuse—
Religious aspects—Christianity.   I. Title.
HV5825.K56   1987   362.2'9   87-12769

ISBN 0-8280-0390-4

Contents

The Quick Fix

With tears streaming down his cheeks, Bob, a 38-year-old alcoholic, struggled to tell his story. He sat in a circle with 16 fellow patients, all in treatment for chemical addiction.

Holding his head in his hands, elbows resting on his knees, Bob seemed to be talking to the floor. "I threw away a good marriage. My wife couldn't put up with my drinking any longer. She left home with our kids six months ago."

The group sat hushed, each patient knew from personal experience how difficult it is to share the pain and loss. The topic under discussion was how the disease of drug addiction destroys the user's value system.

Bob continued. "Here I am today. I've lost everything I treasure—my family, my business, my identity. For what?"

No one responded to his question—it had no answer. Each group member could identify with the insanity of Bob's disease. Each one had settled for less—trading off security, self-esteem, and intimate relationships to feed an insatiable habit—to find the quick fix.

H. L. Mencken once said, "There is a solution to every problem—quick, simple, and wrong." A sizable segment of American society, insanely pursuing the quick chemical fix, refuses to heed Mencken's message of warning.

Chemical addiction is the number one health problem in the United States. Nearly every man, woman, and child has a relative or friend fighting a chemical-abuse problem. Nearly every family physician has patients who are addicted. Every business has employees, every church has parishioners, every social club has members, searching for the quick fix.

An ominous fact is that drugs and alcohol have become the primary means of coping with pain, pressure, and conflict. We Americans—by the millions—use legal and illegal drugs to grapple with the pressures of surviving the eighties. The sinister message that comfort can be found in a pill or a bottle is everywhere. It beckons to us seductively at home and on the street, on TV and the printed page, in the doctor's office and the halls of learning. Each of us is vulnerable to this attractive line.

The frightening result—we have become a nation of addicts. One of every four adults is addicted to legally prescribed drugs—painkillers, diet pills, or sedatives. More than 13.5 million of us are alcoholics. Two and a half million are hooked on cocaine, and 20 million regularly smoke marijuana.

Our nation staggers under the burden of this raging epidemic. Alcohol alone is involved in more than 66 percent of the country's homicides, 50 percent of the rapes, up to 70 percent of the assaults, and 50 percent of the child molestations.

Alcohol is involved in 80 percent of the nation's suicides and is the culprit in 25,000 of the yearly deaths from auto accidents.

Bob angrily pounded his fist into the palm of his hand. "Here I am, 38 years old, and my disease has been out of control since I was 12! I remember the day some of us kids wanted to have a record hop, but we didn't have an amplifier. One of my friends said that St. Teresa's church had a good one in the school hall. So I took a couple of swigs from a bottle of booze and volunteered to steal the amp. Can you believe that, rip off a church? It's insane."

Experts put a $60 billion price tag on the insanity alcohol inflicts yearly on the United States economy. This includes health-care expenses, costs to businesses and property, as well as the financial losses suffered by individuals in connection with death, personal injury, and property damage.

But that's not the end of the carnage. Add to this monstrous waste the obscene squandering of resources caused by the use of illegal drugs such as cocaine, heroin, and marijuana, and the impact soars to more than $100 billion a year. Thirty percent of the nation's prison population are drug addicts. We taxpayers pick up the tab to the tune of $15,000 a year to confine each one. On top of that, health-care rehabilitation costs, the burgeoning incidence of robbery and burglary to support the addicts' habits, and the financial burden of increased law enforcement take a sizable bite out of our wallets.

Tragically, the price of chemical addiction goes

far beyond the damage to our wallets. Who can put a dollar value on the wanton waste of life, the destruction of cherished relationships, and the distortion and disruption of family life?

"I can identify with what Bob's saying." Ellen, a young woman in her late 20s, wiped her eyes nervously with a tissue. She sat next to him in the circle of 16 patients.

"My little girl, Sandy, is 4. She has been in a foster home since she was 5 months old. The Department of Social Services took her away from me. I had no time to care for her. Every day I stole things from department stores and returned them for refunds to buy heroin. That's insane. I thank God I got caught before it was too late for help."

If we listen, we can hear the anguished cries for help coming from the sufferers of this epidemic. They come from abused children of addicted parents, from abandoned spouses, from rape victims, from bereaved families, and from helpless users themselves. If not checked, this relentless disease will take the life of the addict, raise havoc with every family member, disrupt the lives of friends and acquaintances, and jeopardize countless innocent victims.

But there is hope. Chemical addiction is a treatable disease. The resources of medicine, social work, pastoral care, and other agencies are poised to help the abuser and victim. Also, the resources of the federal government are focused on addiction as a major public health problem.

Chemical addiction is a complex issue with many facets. It is a terminal disease to the user and a destructive force to the family. It's a threat to the stability of society, and social stigmas that die hard accompany it. It has unique effects on certain populations. Several drugs used by addicts present special problems in treatment and recovery.

In this book we will look at some of these issues. We all bear the heavy burden of human suffering caused by drug abuse and alcoholism. We can no longer ignore our personal involvement. But before we can become part of the solution, we must learn more about the problem.

Marijuana—A Major Menace

Marijuana kills!

The latest research shatters the notion that using pot is all fun and games. Far from being harmless, it is more dangerous than cigarette smoking. The smoking of marijuana poses a grim health and behavioral threat to the nation's young population.

Patti knew nothing about the hazards of pot smoking when she took her first puff. She began with an occasional joint after school with her sixth-grade friends. The high felt good—and seemed like fun. But in junior high she recalls sneaking a smoke between classes on a fairly regular basis in the restroom. Patti couldn't see it, but marijuana had her hooked before she entered high school.

Marijuana is the most widely used illegal drug among America's high school seniors. Fifty-nine percent have reported using it during their lifetime. A 1982 national survey further showed that 35 percent had tried pot before they had entered high school. One in 18 high school students smoked pot daily.[1]

Prior to the early seventies no systematic studies had examined the effect of marijuana on humans. Users like Patti believed it was harmless.

But results of research conducted over the past several years tell a far different story.

We now know that marijuana smoke contains comparable amounts of most of the destructive components in tobacco: tar, acetone, carbon monoxide, acetaldehyde, and carcinogens (cancer-causing chemicals). But alarmingly, compared to tobacco smoke it has 50 percent more cancer-causing benzanthracene and even greater amounts of other poisons.[2]

Moreover, the studies isolated hazardous chemicals found only in marijuana: THC, the principal mind-altering drug; 60 additional mood-changing compounds; plus a number of lung and throat irritants. And now, through selective growing techniques, much of the pot available on the street contains 10 times the amount of THC as compared with pot of the sixties and seventies.[3]

American marijuana users inhale deeply and retain the smoke in their lungs as long as possible. To get even higher levels of smoke in their lungs, some use smoking devices to increase the pressure. This practice is particularly harmful in the light of a study released in the *New England Journal of Medicine.* This study points out that all plant life contains polonium as a natural by-product of atmospheric fallout. It is in the air we breathe. Burning the leaves of tobacco or marijuana changes polonium to polonium 210, which releases radioactive alpha particles directly into the airways of the lungs. One thousand times more cancer-causing than the gamma radiation of common X-ray machines, alpha radiation is a prime cause of cancer of the lung in tobacco smokers. Potentially, it is more lethal to pot smokers because the smoke is retained in the lungs much longer,[4] exposing the delicate airway tissue to prolonged exposure to radiation.

Chemicals from a single joint of pot remain in the body for as long as a month. Alcohol is water-soluble and leaves the body after several hours. THC, on the other hand, is fat-soluble and is stored for long periods of time in high-fat-content body areas such as the lungs, the brain, and the reproductive organs. Not surprisingly, these are the organs most adversely affected by pot smoking. Growing adolescents and teenagers who smoke during puberty are particularly vulnerable.

Patti's use of marijuana increased to a joint a day during her first year in high school. Her circle of pot-smoking friends grew larger, too. Partying, which by now included a beer or two with a smoke, became a weekly high point. Patti found that schoolwork came harder. She had been a good student through most of her grammar school and junior high years, but now her grades began to tumble. Teachers and parents pressed her to do better. Patti blamed it on tougher subjects, but she couldn't keep up.

Research in brain functioning at UCLA shows how critically marijuana impairs the learning process of growing youngsters.[5] It interferes with the brain's ability to form new memories by causing information gaps in learning. Pot disrupts logical thought. This brings about "magical thinking," where the user believes performance is good, but in reality it is poor. Marijuana keeps the smoker in a state of apathy, taking away the drive to keep up. Consequently, the user loses interest in school and often drops out. The regular smoker, habitually stoned, has little time to develop social skills and cannot practice the growing tasks needed to develop and mature. Finally, pot interrupts the process of affirmation—good grades, praise from adults, feelings of self-worth—which encourages adolescents and teenagers to grow psychologically. These affirmations are replaced by the euphoria of being high—the "quick fix" for pain and pressure.

In her second year of high school Patti's pot smoking caught up with her. A lack of interest in class work, an I-don't-care attitude, and a growing record of unexcused absences caused school authorities to take notice. At the same time, her behavior at home disrupted the family. Frequent confrontations over being out late, several minor driving accidents, increasing drunkenness, and chronically poor health raised her parents' anxiety level. They never knew it, but at one point she thought she might be pregnant. Patti's life became unmanageable.

Pot smoking during puberty is a serious health hazard for young people. Research has demonstrated that in women THC (now in amounts 10 times more potent than the 1970s) reduces the hormones that stimulate ovulation, menstruation, and milk production. In female laboratory rats and mice, THC led to significantly lower fertility rates, especially during puberty. The implications are shocking. If adolescents and teenagers smoke pot long enough, permanent infertility can result.[6]

The THC in marijuana smoke also poses a severe threat to young male smokers. It lowers the level of testosterone, the male sex hormone. This decreases fertility, interferes with sexual development, reduces the size of the testicles, and damages the sperm—a frightening thought for the pot-smoking young men of our nation.

Information concerning the effect of pot smoking on human pregnancy and infants is alarming.[7] One study of pot-smoking mothers revealed five times more premature births than nonsmoking mothers. These babies were prone to problems similar to those marking fetal alcohol syndrome: small body and head size, reduced eye openings, undersized fingernails and toenails. They also had joint movement problems, heart murmurs, and abnormal ears. The studies confirmed the presence of THC in the blood of these infants—even before birth. They were the unwitting victims of pot.

Marijuana also has a devastating effect on the lungs. Studies[8] demonstrate that pot impairs lung function even more than does the use of tobacco. Pot smokers, according to these studies, develop symptoms of acute bronchitis more quickly than do heavy tobacco smokers. This research revealed that 18- to 21-year-old users were developing abnormal precancerous cells in their lung tissue—a condition that would take heavy tobacco smokers 10 to 20 years to produce. Also, people who smoke both pot and tobacco dramatically increase the risk of developing chronic bronchitis, emphysema, and lung cancer.[9]

The National Household Survey[10] indicates that 3 million adolescents and teenagers and 17 million adults regularly use marijuana. The implications of these facts point ominously to a potential epidemic of lung cancer, chronic obstructive pulmonary disease, and other pot-induced problems within the next 5 to 10 years. Add this impending disaster to the major health problems created by tobacco smoking, and the future health of our nation's youth seems bleak.

Though eager to learn how to drive, Patti had difficulty in developing good driving skills. Her minor auto accidents prompted her parents to restrict her use of the family car. One of her friends suffered a severe injury in an alcohol/pot-related auto accident. As a result, Patti's parents dreaded to answer the phone when she partied at night—it might be a hospital emergency room calling to inform them that their daughter had been in an accident. Patti was fortunate. The school authorities sensed the problem she struggled with and intervened by contacting her parents. Together they got her into treatment for her addiction. Three weeks in an addiction treatment unit were not easy. Withdrawal from an addictive substance is difficult, and marijuana is no exception. Moreover, Patti's alcohol use only made it harder. She soon learned that she had an addictive disease and must make significant lifestyle changes to cope with it. Caring parents and supportive teachers helped her through treatment. With their help she turned her life around.

But what about the other 20 million pot smokers? Marijuana is a major health menace to American young people. This menace is rapidly approaching epidemic proportions. If you smoke pot—get smart—quit before it is too late. If you're hooked and can't stop on your own, get help. It is as close as your nearest hospital. Most have referral services that can put you in touch with resources to help you quit.

Unfortunately, pot smoking usually leads to an even greater problem—mixing pot with alcohol.

Endnotes

[1] "Marijuana and the Lungs," *American Thoracic Society News,* Winter 1984.

[2] Hoffman, Brunneman, Gori, et al., "On the Carcinogenicity of Marijuana Smoke," *Recent Advances in Phytochemistry* 9 (1975): 63-81.

[3] "Marijuana and the Lungs."

[4] D. Tashkin et al., "Subacute Effects of Heavy Marijuana on Pulmonary Function in Healthy Men," *New England Journal of Medicine* 294:125-129.

[5] R. G. Heath, *Marijuana and the Brain* (New York: American Council on Marijuana and Other Psychoactive Drugs, 1981).

[6] "Marijuana and Reproduction," *Marijuana, a Second Look* (New York: American Lung Association, 1984).

[7] *Ibid.*

[8] F. S. Tennant et al., "Medical Manifestations Associated With Hashish," *Journal of the American Medical Association* 216 (1971): 1965-1969.

[9] D. Tashkin and S. Cohen, *Marijuana and Its Effects on the Lungs* (New York: American Council on Marijuana and Other Psychoactive Drugs, 1981), p. 31.

[10] "Current Drug Use, March 30, 1984, National Household Survey," *NIDA Capsule,* March 1984.

Alcohol and Pot—A Deadly Combination

"You old folks guzzle your booze, we'll smoke pot." This teenage taunt, hurled repeatedly at the establishment in the seventies, isn't heard much anymore.

Marijuana, once a symbol of youthful dissent, is now mixed with alcohol by the pot-smoking crew for a bigger kick. This lethal blend poses a serious threat to the health and safety of user and nonuser alike.

John arrived at the addictions center directly from court. The police arrested him at the scene of a one-car accident in which his sister was killed. The initial charge was "driving under the influence." He blew a .15 on the Breathalyzer and spent the night in jail.

At the arraignment next morning, the judge ordered immediate treatment before disposition of the case. Further tests at the treatment center revealed that he was also under the influence of pot.

John's case is typical. Alcohol and marijuana are the most commonly used in combination of nonmedical, recreational drugs in society today. National surveys[1] show that an alarming 56 percent of current alcohol users routinely smoke pot, and of the 20 million Americans who smoke pot as their drug of choice, most also regularly drink alcohol. These statistics are foreboding because 13.5 million of us, including 3 million adolescents, are already problem drinkers.

When these two psychochemicals are used together—which is an increasingly common practice—their individual effects add to each other. The degree of intoxication is increased and lasts longer. In fact, the "kick" from alcohol/pot not only lasts longer; it is 135 percent greater than getting high on alcohol alone and 20 percent greater than using pot alone. This common street knowledge has now been confirmed in the laboratory.[2]

This lethal mixture is made even more powerful now that pot, as pointed out before, contains 10 times more THC than the pot of the sixties and the seventies. We are all victims of this witch's brew, a concoction that contributes to the major behavioral problems that pervade society today.

Distorted behavior of millions of users is the result. Manual skills and mental abilities are crippled, creating hazardous effects on performance of complex tasks such as driving motor vehicles, flying airplanes, operating machinery, and making complicated decisions.

This frightening reality leads directly to a major problem. In addition to the nation's alcohol driving mess, we are now confronted with a rapidly growing alcohol/pot driving menace. In a California Department of Justice survey[3] of 1,800 drivers arrested for operating a motor vehicle while intoxicated, 14 percent were found to have THC in their urine. Two thirds (168) of these drivers tested positive to alcohol as well. The clear message of these statistics is: driving on America's highways is hazardous to your health. It is frightening to know that at least 10 percent of the drivers on our roads are under the influence of both alcohol and pot. Moreover, these persons mistakenly believe they are good drivers.

A recent survey among high school students[4] revealed that many teens believe alcohol and pot cancel out the negative effects of the other. They are convinced that using the two drugs in combination actually makes complex tasks, including driving an automobile, easier. Nothing could be further from the truth. The most extensive investigation into the combined behavioral effect of alcohol and pot has been in the operation of motor vehicles.[5] Driving skills impaired by this mixture include: glare recovery, manual dexterity, visual signal perception, peripheral vision, and divided attention. Research demonstrates that the combination of these two drugs produces greater impairment than either drug alone.

These studies clearly show that the negative effects of alcohol and pot reach beyond driving skills. The disturbing conclusion: millions of Americans are living gravely crippled lives. They are functioning at levels dangerously below their potential.

That's not all the abuser of these two drugs faces. Cross-tolerance—where the alcoholic needs more pot to get high, and vice versa—occurs between these chemicals. This sets the stage for double addiction and extensive physical disease.

Cross-tolerance causes prolonged exposure of the body to high concentrations of alcohol and marijuana. Despite the fact that alcohol is water soluble and leaves the body in a few hours, high levels in the body severely damage vital organ systems. This erupts in illnesses such as gastritis, liver disease, pancreatitis, and heart disease. If these high levels go unchecked, permanent disability or death often results.

THC, the active ingredient in pot, on the other hand, is fat-soluble and is stored for long periods of time in high-fat-content body organs like the brain, heart, and liver. Latest findings[6] show that sustained, elevated amounts of THC in these organs produce increases in metabolism and heart rate. High levels also restrict oxygen delivery to the body and thus limit physical activity. Marijuana smoke obstructs the airways of the lungs, resulting in crippling respiratory disease, lung cancer, and emphysema.[7]

Alcohol and pot used together is a deadly combination that devastates the total person physically, psychologically, and spiritually. John would testify to that.

Treatment for double addiction is tough, and John wasn't prepared for the struggle. Withdrawal from alcohol and pot is painful and frustrating— marked by anxiety, insomnia, irritability, fuzzy thinking, paranoia, and physical and emotional pain.

He faced two different sets of withdrawal symptoms and withdrawal time frames. Acutely ill, John demanded expert medical management. He required alert observation, monitoring of vital signs—pulse, blood pressure, and temperature—and a carefully prepared and followed treatment plan.

Grief and guilt springing from the death of his sister added the spiritual dimension to the physical and psychological problems associated with cross-addiction. John had no idea his life could be so disrupted by the combined use of alcohol and pot. Unfortunately, he learned too late of the devastating effect these two drugs have on unsuspecting victims.

The grim reality is that users of these drugs place themselves at a serious disadvantage because of severe behavioral impairment. Most of the jobs in our society require learning, hand-eye coordination, the ability to remember, logical thinking, and other similarly complex functions. Tasks that demand involved actions, such as driving a motor vehicle, suffer most from the alcohol/pot combination. This is not only a forbidding threat to abusers like John but also a frightening menace to the public at large.

Abusers of this deadly mixture—among whom are operators of public transport, law enforcement officers, public officials, professionals in health care—threaten the public safety. This danger is evident in the rising frequency of drug-related bus and railroad accidents, airline near misses, medical malpractice suits, and corruption of public officials.

It appears obvious that nonusers must play a more active role in the war against drug abuse. This menace touches each person. Concerned family members, friends, professionals in whatever role, have a responsibility to act on the earliest symptoms of drug abuse displayed by those close to us. Denial of the problem only delays treatment. In fact, by refusing to confront drug abuse, we enable the victim to continue on a self-destructive course that inevitably leads to disaster.

John's case is a shocking example. Successful treatment was not the end of the pain and disruption caused by his addiction to alcohol and pot. After release from the treatment center, John still faced the court system. Charged with vehicular manslaughter and driving while intoxicated, he spent some time in jail.

Drug addiction is a crippling disease, affecting user and nonuser alike. Let's look at another dimension of this life-threatening epidemic—the nightmare of heroin.

Endnotes

[1] "Current Drug Use, March 30, 1984, National Household Survey," *NIDA Capsule,* March 1984.

[2] L. R. Sutton, "The Effects of Alcohol, Marijuana, and Their Combination on Driving Ability," *Journal of Studies on Alcohol* 44, No. 3 (1983).

[3] V. C. Reeve, "Incidence of Marijuana in a California

Impaired Driver Population," Sacramento, State of California, Department of Justice, Division of Law Enforcement, Investigative Service Branch, 1979.

[4] L. R. Sutton, "Alcohol and Marijuana Use and Attitudes Towards Driving in a Rural Secondary County," unpublished manuscript, 1981.

[5] S. Cohen and P. Lessin, "Marijuana and Alcohol," Neuropsychiatric Institute Center for the Health Sciences, University of California at Los Angeles, 1982.

[6] R. G. Heath, *Marijuana and the Brain* (New York: The American Council on Marijuana and Other Psychoactive Drugs, 1981).

[7] Tennant, "Medical Manifestations Associated With Hashish."

Heroin—A Nightmare Come True

Heroin is a nightmare beyond description. The hardest of drugs. The toughest monkey for anyone to get off his back."

- A youth in a ghetto shooting gallery makes a connection, mainlines, and OD's himself to an early grave.
- A street pusher tries to sell heroin to children on the steps of a church after Mass.
- A teenager in a fashionable Boston suburb injects a bad dose of heroin and falls dead, the syringe still stuck in his arm.

These are scenes all too familiar in America's world of heroin addiction. No longer headline news, they are commonplace events on the street.

Chemical addiction is the nation's number-one health problem. And heroin is its most frightening manifestation.[1] It is a terrifying drug, distorting and twisting its healthiest users into diseased and grotesquely misshapen wrecks. Heroin robs them of all human dignity, finally snatching away the last gasp of life. Like a malignant cancer, it spreads through respectable neighborhoods, reducing them to scattered rubble and gutted tenements inhabited by "hopheads," the street name of heroin addicts.

Heroin siphons billions of dollars each year from our treasuries—for law enforcement, for treatment programs, for heroin-related diseases that burden our health-care system. "Junk" saps our national spirit by wasting lives, demoralizing communities, and terrifying our citizens into living behind dead-bolted and triple-locked doors.[2]

Heroin comes from the opium poppy. Its active ingredient is morphine, an addictive narcotic that has been used since the Civil War as a painkiller. Pharmacists at the turn of the century sold it in over-the-counter tonics and nostrums guaranteed to cure all sorts of illnesses. As a result, thousands of Americans became addicted to the drug.

Because of this, the search began for a nonaddictive painkiller. Diacetylmorphine, produced from morphine by a process called acetylation, was heralded as the ideal substitute. As a painkiller, it is more powerful than morphine. And it was thought to be nonaddictive. But the early optimism crumbled in the face of the grim reality—it was even more addictive than morphine. The popular name for diacetylmorphine is heroin.

This drug has a profound effect on mood. Users describe it as thrilling and relaxing, relieving worry and giving a heightened sense of well-being. But addiction quickly follows the first shot. Repeated use creates physical tolerance in which the user must take larger and larger doses to get the same high. Once hooked, the addict can't stop without experiencing withdrawal symptoms. Heroin highs are short, so users often have to take it four to six times a day to avoid the screaming and sweating agonies of withdrawal—nausea, stomach cramps, and severe depression.

Addicts in the United States use heroin in several ways. They snuff it (like cocaine, it is easily absorbed through nasal membranes). They inject it under the skin (commonly called "skin-popping"). But the preferred method is injecting the drug intravenously ("mainlining").

First heating the white powder and converting it to a liquid, the addict injects it into a primary vein. A sudden rush of euphoria, which some users consider better than an orgasm, sweeps through the body. This is followed by a mellower period, a high that lasts for several hours.

Abusers clumsily shoot up their bodies with dirty needles and ineptly heated heroin, causing abscesses, hepatitis, and collapsed veins. Dazed, disoriented, and desperate for a fix, they inject their legs, feet, arms, and even their tongue, neck, and groin. They have only one goal—to get heroin into their bloodstream—to keep the high going.

Society commonly assumes that heroin abuse is limited to Blacks and Hispanics living in ghetto communities. Heroin addiction does run rampant in the poverty-stricken inner city, but it has also become entrenched in middle-class suburbs across America.[3]

Middle-class heroin users have until recently been an invisible population. They were seldom arrested and usually got help from their family physician rather than from drug-treatment centers. In the early stages of addiction, they could continue to function close to normal as long as they had access to clean heroin and they used disposable needles. But nearly everyone who toys with heroin winds up seriously addicted.

A young high-tech engineer gave vivid testimony of his struggle with heroin. "When I began experimenting with heroin, I never believed I would become an addict."

The young professional sat in a circle with other persons who had come to a community substance-abuse center for treatment. You could see the pain in his eyes. The hurt was evident in his faltering voice as he continued. "It didn't seem possible. I have a good position and everything I could want. But I got the shock of my life the other morning when I woke up with a runny nose, chills, and a fever. I was going through withdrawal—I was addicted to heroin!"

Luckily the engineer still had the good sense to get help, rather than another fix. Through uncommon personal effort and the boundless support of staff and fellow patients in the treatment center, the young man broke his dependency on heroin.

"It was the most difficult thing I ever did in my life," he later admitted.

Treatment for heroin addiction is no easy road to follow. The drug is an efficient painkiller, and more important, the heroin high is pleasant. Non-users of drugs generally regard junkies as crazed and suicidal thrill-seekers. No one except the user understands what drives him to stick a needle into his arm. But the addict knows—the euphoria and bliss of morphine. Opium has tempted the human race for 3,000 years or more. Anyone who has received an injection of morphine, Demerol, or codeine (all derivatives of opium) in a hospital after an operation knows the bliss the drug can give. The high is pleasant, but it will ruin your life and probably kill you. Nevertheless, it is the high that makes it difficult to treat heroin addiction. It is very hard to turn one's back on the euphoria of the high.

The most successful treatment programs[4] start with the premise that heroin is a chronic, life-threatening disease. Like those suffering from other chronic illnesses, such as diabetes and hypertension, the victim must be prepared to treat it the rest of his life. Nothing short of such a commitment will work. After initial intervention—detoxification and inpatient treatment—the addict must maintain a strong aftercare support system to stay straight. This means regular involvement with Narcotics Anonymous and a steady sponsor. If the abuser has a family, each member should become involved with NARANON, a support group for the families of drug users.

Another drug contributing to this madness is cocaine—a bosom buddy of heroin and just as destructive and dangerous. It is the topic of chapter five.

Endnotes

[1] J. A. Califano, The 1982 Report on Drug Abuse and Alcoholism (New York: Warner Books, 1982), p. 11.

[2] L. P. Silverman and N. Spruill, "Urban Crime and the Price of Heroin," *Journal of Urban Economics* 4 (1977).

[3] J. Garabedian, *Drugs and the Young* (New York: Tower Publishers, 1970), p. 84.

[4] D. Simpson et al., *Data Book on Drug Treatment Outcomes* (Fort Worth, Tex.: Texas Christian University, Institute of Behavioral Research, 1978).

Cocaine—Instant Insanity

Lights flashing, siren screaming, the ambulance skidded to a stop at the emergency room entrance. Waiting medics rushed a 17-year-old youth into the crisis center. They struggled heroically to revive him, but it was too late.

He and a fellow student were playing cocaine roulette in the high school restroom—first one to drop after sniffing a line of coke would lose the game. The winner went back to his class, leaving the 17-year-old convulsing on the restroom floor. In a minute he was dead.

Cocaine is like that—unpredictable and deadly.

Nicknamed the "champagne of drugs," "gold dust," "the Cadillac of chemicals," and "the gift of the sun god," coke has the reputation of being harmless, nonaddictive, and the recreational drug of choice of the rich.

But supplies have multiplied and prices have dropped. Blue-collar workers, suburban housewives, high school students, middle managers, and street people have joined the wealthy. Cocaine is now used widely at all levels of society.

National surveys[1] indicate that 25 million Americans have tried cocaine, 6 million use it at least once a month, and 2 million are hooked on the drug. Dr. Arnold Washton, director of research of the 800-COCAINE national hotline, says, "There's no question that we're experiencing a cocaine epidemic."

The magnitude of this epidemic is seen in the growth of cocaine-related emergency-room admissions and deaths. These have shot up more than 200 percent in the past five years, according to statistics from the Centers for Disease Control.[2] Unpredictability of the fatal dosage is the prime reason for this dramatic increase.

Dr. Charles V. Wetli, deputy chief medical examiner of Dade County, Florida, says, "Some people have died after ingesting as little as 20 milligrams of cocaine; others have ingested more than a gram and survived. Like any other street drug, a fatal overdose may happen with the user's first cocaine experience, but it is the abuser who is at greatest risk."[3]

Typically, the cocaine reaction (fatal overdose) begins with a normal high, followed by a short period of depression. Suddenly the coke abuser develops convulsions, and death occurs within a matter of minutes.

Music of the drug culture reflects this always-present menace. The Grateful Dead sang a song called "Casey Jones," which talks about the trouble in store for Casey Jones, who had been getting high on cocaine.

Victims of another type of cocaine-related death are showing up with increasing frequency at hospital emergency rooms across the country. Coke-induced psychotic attacks are taking the lives of chronic abusers who have no previous psychiatric history. Otherwise healthy people are experiencing what seem to be paranoid-schizophrenic disorders from which they never recover. These victims undergo an excited state of mental confusion that builds up to unbelievably weird conduct. Fueled by high fever (up to 108° F) and severe paranoia, the abusers create such a ruckus that they must be subdued by the police. In minutes they abruptly stop breathing and die.

It matters little if death follows a whopping overdose or a cocaine-induced frenzy, by the time the user senses trouble, it's usually too late.

That's what makes coke such an unpredictable killer.

Cocaine is no respecter of persons, indiscriminately killing both street people and celebrities like basketball star Len Bias and football star Don Rogers.

Cocaine, a white, odorless alkaloid powder derived from the South American coca plant (not to be confused with cocoa), has a checkered history. South American Indians chew coca leaves to relieve fatigue, suppress appetite, and increase productivity. Before the turn of the century, Europeans spiked their wine with cocaine. Freud recommended it for depression. Americans drank cocaine in the original Coca-Cola until federal law prohibited the use of coca leaves in 1906. Finally in 1914 cocaine was classified as a narcotic and banned from nonmedical use.

Today it is smuggled into the United States 90 to 100 percent pure. But in passing through many hands, it is stepped on (diluted) at every stage with substances such as sugar, heroin, local anesthetics, and amphetamines to increase each dealer's profit.

Anywhere from 1 to 95 percent pure, this chancy chemical creates havoc for the user. Cocaine substitutes and adulterants increase the risk of an already dangerous drug. Not only causing serious physical problems on their own, these substances are the reason coke is so dangerous to use. They make it impossible for the user to keep track of the amount of coke taken.

Adding to the menace of this drug are erroneous but widespread myths and misconceptions that keep alive the idea that cocaine is safe to use.

Most dangerous is the belief that the safe way to take coke is snorting it through the nose. Misguided users feel that by refusing to free-base smoke or mainline coke they protect themselves from addiction and other adverse effects that result from rapid absorbtion into the bloodstream.

The truth is, 60 to 70 percent of those who come into treatment centers for cocaine-related problems snort the drug. A significant number of these die.[4] There is no doubt that dangerous levels of cocaine build up in the bloodstream from this method of abuse.

Recent research[5] shows that pregnant women who snort cocaine may develop premature separation of the placenta, a complication that can kill the fetus. A 19-year-old woman, 7 months pregnant, was rushed to the hospital with vaginal bleeding and contractions several hours after snorting coke. Following an emergency Cesarean section, she delivered a stillborn infant. Physicians found a large clot of blood behind the placenta. This is typical of the information recent research has uncovered.

Another myth, widely popularized by the media, holds that free-base smoking is less dangerous than other ways of using coke. It is believed that the free-base process purges the toxic chemical impurities from the cocaine. In reality, free-base smokers are at greater risk from poisonous reactions, pulmonary problems, and death from cocaine.[6] Providing the swiftest access to the bloodstream, free-based cocaine is rapidly absorbed by the lungs and within seconds is carried to the brain and the central nervous system. The high peaks almost instantly. But it's short-lived, lasting only 15 to 30 minutes. Users often go on "cocaine binges," taking the drug again and again for hours—sometimes days—to stretch out the high.

Without fail "cocaine crashes" follow "cocaine binges." Abusers try to relieve the paranoia, depression, restlessness, and irritability by using other drugs—alcohol, heroin, and sedatives—to ease the crash. But they wind up suffering the serious effects of cross-addiction. They become addicted to two or more drugs at the same time.

This brings us to the third misconception, the belief that cocaine is not addicting. Addiction develops directly from the struggle to avoid the cocaine crash. More coke gets the addict out of depression, and the stage is set for chronic compulsive abuse.[7]

It's the repetitive use of coke that ensnares the

abuser in the morass of addiction. After prolonged, heavy cocaine abuse, the pleasant effects of the drug give way to apathy and depression. Not even more coke can then throw off the cocaine blues, which Dave Van Ronk sang about in 1960.

Many abusers, however, try to conquer the cocaine blues by moving on to free-base smoking and mainlining. The end result is the same as with any other addictive drug—heroin, alcohol, or amphetamines—total disruption of one's personal, social, and professional life.

They're hooked!

Beating fatigue and depression with coke becomes the addict's overwhelming obsession. The Leadbelly musical group sang about this obsession in their song "Take a Whiff on Me." The lyrics tell about an addict who knows what the doctors say about the lethal quality of cocaine, but the junkie will continue snorting cocaine until it kills him.

Relief from this deadly spiral can come only through total and permanent abstinence from cocaine. Coke victims must accept their reality: they are helpless, their lives are out of control, they have a terminal illness, and the cause of it all is cocaine.

Cocaine's destructive power ravaged the life of a young mother. Her disease progressed from occasional recreational use of coke to a disastrously expensive addiction. She ultimately sold her 5-month-old baby girl to finance her habit.

When abusers accept their powerlessness over cocaine and see that life has become unmanageable, *then* they are in a position to get help. The three most effective methods for treatment of cocaine addiction are: 1. Join a support group like Cocaine Anonymous or Coke Enders. 2. Become a member of a recognized outpatient substance-abuse program. 3. Be admitted to an inpatient addictions-treatment program.

Concerned family and friends can help best by getting the victim to a certified substance-abuse counselor. The professional will make the proper referral to the appropriate treatment source. Cocaine addiction is a chronic, lifelong illness with a high probability of relapse. For this reason continuity of care, featuring a strong, active support system—understanding family members, psychological counseling focusing on support, and a congenial and restful setting—is vital for recovery.

Returning control of life back to the victim is the ultimate goal of treatment. External rules and guidelines are useful tools during treatment, but in the end, recovery results when the user develops the ability to live without chemical crutches.

The "champagne of drugs" enjoys an extraordinary popularity. On the one hand, it appears to offer excitement, euphoria, and escape from depression. It holds out the promise to make the unbearable seem bearable. But on the other hand, it demands a stiff price—physical disease, insanity, compromised spiritual values, addiction, and death.

Don't let the nicknames fool you. Cocaine is a killer.

When the uninitiated look into the world of illicit drugs, they have feelings of helplessness and fear. Yet there is a new angle to this frightening scene that causes great concern among those who are fighting the war against these chemical killers—designer drugs. In the next chapter we will see how drug pushers are using legal means to sell their killer concoctions.

Endnotes

[1] "NIDA 1982 National Survey on Drug Abuse," Rockville, Md., NIDA.

[2] "Cocaine Out of Control," *Emergency Medicine,* Sept. 30, 1984, p. 79.

[3] *Ibid.*

[4] "NIDA 1979 National Survey on Drug Abuse," Rockville, Md., NIDA; B. S. Finckle and K. L. McCloskey, "The Forensic Toxicology of Cocaine," *Cocaine 1977 NIDA Research Monogram* 13.

[5] D. Acker et al., "Abruptia Placentae Associated With Cocaine Use," *American Journal of Obstetrics and Gynecology* 146 (May 1983): 220-221.

[6] J. Itkonen et al., "Pulmonary Dysfunction in Free-Base Cocaine Users," *Archives of Internal Medicine* (in press).

[7] S. H. Schnoll, "Cocaine Dependence," *Resident and Staff Physician* 30, No. 11 (Nov. 1984): 24-31.

Designer Drugs

It looks like heroin. It's packaged like heroin. It costs like heroin. And it kicks like heroin. But this drug sure isn't heroin.

Made to look and act like heroin but concocted in an underground lab, this heroin-like drug is dangerous, mind-bending, and entirely legal.

Any resemblance between this brew and the real stuff is strictly intentional.

It is one of a number of designer drugs churned out by clandestine chemists across the United States. These pharmacologists create customized drugs by subtly varying the chemical structure of an existing drug. Until it is detected and banned by the United States Drug Enforcement Administration, the designer drug is legal to make, sell, and use.

When the Drug Enforcement Administration does bar it, the underground chemist designs a new—and legal—variation. United States law requires the DEA to act after the fact, so the underground chemists are always one step ahead of law enforcement.

This new twist in drug abuse is creating a windfall for drug dealers. In the first place, the dangerous operations required to import illegal drugs from outside the United States are elimi-

nated. In the second place, a mere $500 invest-
ment in raw materials is enough to cook up a
supply of drugs worth $2 million on the street—
and it's legal. All that's needed is minimal lab
equipment and a pharmacologist capable of making the stuff from a recipe.

Designer drugs are not new but date back to LSD
in the mid-1960s. Now, however, it is a far more
sophisticated process. These drugs are
tailor-made, both in potency and in duration of
the high.

Clandestine chemists focus on legal, synthetic
narcotics that act like heroin, such as Sublimaze, a
surgical anesthetic.[1] By slightly altering the chemical structure of the legal drug, the pharmacist
produces street drugs known as China White,
Persian White, Adam, Ecstasy, Mexican Brown, or
some other underground street tag.

Odds for the unwary user taking a lethal overdose from these new heroin-like brews are great.
Designer drugs are as much as 3,000 times more
potent than heroin bought on the street.[2] But even
more ominous are the growing numbers of users
suffering from a Parkinson's-like paralysis. Lethal
MPTP, a contaminant discovered in designer
drugs, has been linked to neurologic disorders,
paralysis, brain damage, and death among the
users of this new breed of drugs.

With the word out on the street about the
dangers of these new drugs, more and more victims are showing up at clinics. They complain of
stiffness, impaired speech, rigidity, and tremors.
A number, usually brought in by friends or rela-

tives, suffer from severe paralysis.

Alert researchers recognized these complaints as symptomatic of Parkinson's disease. The users were treated quite successfully with L-dopa, the medication used to treat persons suffering from Parkinson's disease.

But the disturbing element is that Parkinson's disease develops with normal aging, striking the elderly almost exclusively. The symptoms don't appear until one has lost 80 percent of the cells in the *substantia nigra*, the center of the brain that produces dopamine, a neurotransmitter. These young users of designer drugs probably have lost 50 percent of their *substantia nigra* cells after using only two or three doses. Experts close to this problem fear that we will be seeing a wave of Parkinson's cases among young people in the coming years.

But in spite of the lethal side effects of these potent powders, illicit chemists continue to concoct new brews that are eagerly snapped up on the streets. The DEA has shut down more than 1,500 clandestine labs, and Congress may soon take broader action against designer drugs, but it might be too little, too late.

Given the enormous profits to be made and the ingenious schemes that keep underground drug designers one step ahead of the law, it's only a matter of time before this becomes a catastrophic national health problem.

In case you think that because you don't use alcohol or pot and because you would never take a hard drug like heroin or cocaine, you're not a part of the problem—think again. In chapter seven we will look at tranquilizers. It's possible that you are one of the millions hooked on prescribed pills.

Endnotes

[1] J. Shafer, "Designer Drugs," *Science*, March 1985, pp. 60-67.

[2] R. Schulman and M. Sabin, "The Losing War Against 'Designer Drugs,'" *Business Week*, June 24, 1985, pp. 101-104.

The "Harmless" but Deadly Tranquilizers

Are you hooked on a "harmless" pill?

Millions of Americans are and don't know it. You could be one of them!

Writhing on the hospital bed, the woman was obviously suffering intense pain. During moments of lucidness her terror became evident.

"It's like fire burning all over my skin. It's agony," she gasped.

Twenty-four hours earlier she had been rushed unconscious and barely alive to the emergency room of a suburban hospital. Apparently she was another drug-overdose victim. Instead, she was just the opposite—seven days earlier she had quit taking Valium.

Vivian is one of 8,000 persons admitted yearly to emergency rooms across the United States for Valium addiction. She is typical of tens of thousands of her fellow Americans who use the drug. Prescribed initially for depression following the death of her mother, her daily dosage of Valium began at 15 milligrams. Four and a half years later she was using 40 milligrams a day. Fearing addiction, Vivian decided to stop.

Every year more than 4,500 people enter drug

treatment centers for the first time for addiction to minor tranquilizers.[1] National Institute for Drug Abuse statistics indicate that this is only the tip of the iceberg. Many millions of Americans using Valium and other members of the benzodiazepine family of drugs are not aware of their addiction. Consequently, they have made no effort to quit.[2] Ominously, clinical studies show that doses of the benzodiazepines as low as 10 milligrams per day for a period of four months can be addictive.[3]

The benzodiazepine family of so-called minor tranquilizers is divided into two groups. A longer-acting group includes Centrax, Dalmane, Librium, Tranxene, and Valium. The shorter-acting group includes Ativan, Halcion, Restoril, and Serax. While the shorter-acting drugs are less likely to accumulate to dangerous levels, they may produce more dramatic withdrawal symptoms if dependency develops. Unsupervised withdrawal, such as Vivian's, from any of the drugs in this family is dangerous.

Vivian experienced seven days of hell after quitting cold turkey: terrifying hallucinations, severe muscle constrictions, and sleep and appetite disturbances. She ultimately lost consciousness, went into convulsions, and ended up in the hospital to face the rigors of detoxification. The torturous burning sensations she experienced are common to withdrawal from the use of the benzodiazepines.

Using any of these drugs is a risky trade-off at best, with only a few benefits but many side effects. For instance, an August 1983, trade statement publicizing one of the most recent additions to the benzodiazepine family suggests Halcion as "useful for short-term management of insomnia, with common adverse reactions similar to those of other benzodiazepines, such as drowsiness, dizziness, mild incoordination, headache, gastrointestinal upset, and paradoxical reactions such as stimulation, agitation, sleep disturbances, and hallucinations."[4] These are not the most severe side effects either. United States Drug Enforcement Administration (DEA) statistics show that hundreds of people die yearly as a result of taking benzodiazepines, primarily because of accidental overdose when used with alcohol or other drugs.[5]

Users of this family of drugs risk other serious hazards: attacks of hostility and rage, extreme confusion, birth defects, and other problems in newborn infants.[6]

In spite of conflicting data concerning the effectiveness of these tranquilizers, the American public has been subjected to significant pressure to use them to cope with high levels of tension and stress. Using intense and skillful marketing techniques aimed at physicians, the drug-manufacturing companies have capitalized on the heightened anxiety of the average American. Doctors are urged to prescribe one of the benzodiazepines as an appropriate response to all manner of personal and social stressors.[7]

Such clients as "frustrated housewives, students apprehensive about unstable world and national conditions, a demanding or complaining patient," and older people who "face constraints brought about by reduced capabilities" are suggested by the manufacturers as likely candidates for the drug.[8]

The shocking result: 70 million prescriptions filled yearly, which translates into 3.6 billion pills. Despite the risk tranquilizers bring to the elderly (confusion and the likelihood of being branded as senile, sleep apnea—episodes of not breathing while asleep—and danger from interaction with other drugs), the pressure is on physicians to extend these drugs further into the lucrative market of older Americans.[9] Today more than 44 percent of the users of these drugs are over 60.

Janet, an attractive senior citizen, was admitted to a hospital psychiatric unit for depression, anxiety, severe headaches, and lack of motivation. With the preliminary diagnosis of major depression, she did not respond to the usual treatment of medication and psychotherapy. An alert psychiatrist suspected chemical addiction and transferred her to the addictions treatment unit for detoxification.

She had begun taking prescribed Librium 10 years previously as treatment for depression following the death of her husband. When she was admitted to the hospital, she was using 40 milligrams a day. On several occasions she had wanted to quit, but her physician encouraged her to continue.

Most people—including many physicians—do not realize that taking the usually prescribed dosage of tranquilizers can result in addiction. Several studies show that low doses of these drugs may be the major source of addiction. In a 1979 United States Food and Drug Administration report, 82 percent of persons addicted to benzodiazepines were taking doses in the usually prescribed ranges.[10]

As early as 1969 Dr. Jerome Levine, of the National Institute of Mental Health, warned that addiction to low doses of these tranquilizers was a serious problem.[11] The British medical journal *Lancet* reported that low doses of Valium taken for as short a period as four months could produce severe withdrawal symptoms.[12] It is possible to become addicted even when carefully following a physician's instructions.

The sobering truth is that Janet and Vivian represent hundreds of thousands of Americans who are in grave danger. Perilously ignorant of the threat of chemical addiction, the American public has been victimized by a drug problem approaching epidemic proportions. DEA statistics confirm that Valium is the number-one drug involving emergency room visits. During 1980 there were 6,000 Valium-related visits. The entire benzodiazepine family of drugs was involved in more than 25,000 visits. Heroin and morphine, the next most commonly abused drugs, lagged well behind with 8,600 visits to emergency rooms.[13] If you have been using one of these drugs longer than several months, you may be hooked. Several warning signs can alert you to the danger:

1. Are you taking more pills to get the same effect? Continued use can cause increased toler-

ance for the drug, developing the need for more than the prescribed amount to get the same effect.

2. Do you need the drug? If you can't cope without your daily dose, the drug has become a crutch.

3. Can you quit without discomfort? Withdrawal symptoms such as headaches, tension, nervousness, and the shakes may develop when you quit. If the symptoms disappear when you resume using the pills, you're probably hooked.

If these warning signs characterize your use of tranquilizers, you're probably one of the millions of Americans hooked on a "harmless" pill. Don't make the same mistake Vivian did by quitting cold turkey. Get professional help from a physician familiar with the process of withdrawal from the benzodiazepines.

That "harmless" pill could be deadly.

Endnotes

[1] "National Institute on Drug Abuse, 1980 Data From the Client Data Acquisition Process Series E, No. 21," U.S. Department of Health and Human Services, July 1981.

[2] L. Burke et al., "Benzodiazepines: Extent and Character of Use," unpublished draft, U.S. Food and Drug Administration, Oct. 18, 1979.

[3] P. Tyrer et al., "Benzodiazepine Withdrawal Symptoms and Propranolol," *The Lancet* (1981): 520-522.

[4] J. R. Hagstrom, R.Ph., "Halcion-A, New Agent for Insomnia," *Pharmacy Capsule*, August 1983.

[5] "Drug Abuse Warning Network, 1980 Annual Report DEA, Contract No. 81-3," U.S. Drug Enforcement Administration, 1981.

[6] D. J. Greenblatt and R. I. Shader, "Benzodiazepines," *New England Journal of Medicine* 291 (1974): 1239-1243.

[7] Hoffman-LaRoche, 1975, 1981 mailings to physicians.

[8] U.S., Cong., Senate, Subcommittee on Monopoly of the Senate Select Committee on Small Business, *Effects of Promotion and Advertising of Over the Counter Drugs on Competition, Small Business, and the Health and Welfare of the Public,* part 2, Hearing, 92nd Cong., 1st sess. (1971), p. 546.

[9] Hoffman-LaRoche, "The Later Years: An Optimistic Outlook," 1979 mailing to physicians.

[10] United States Food and Drug report, 1979.

[11] *Ibid.*

[12] Drug Abuse Warning Network, 1980.

[13] *Ibid.*

Additional Reference

Levine, J. Statement before the Senate Subcommittee on Monopoly. Quoted in *FDC Reports,* July 21, 1969, p. 7.

Addiction—A Family Disease

Chemical addiction tears the family apart. It angers, confuses, bewilders, and frightens every member. Unable to escape or ignore the bizarre behavior, they are forced to interact daily with their addicted loved one. As a result, the family members become coaddicted, often as sick as the user.

Between sobs the 18-year-old girl confronted her father, Tom. "Most of my life I believed you didn't love me. You paid me no attention." She paused, wiped the tears from her cheeks, and then continued. "I thought I wasn't wanted. When I got older, you embarrassed me so many times in front of my friends that I stopped inviting them home because of your drinking."

Tom listened quietly while his family, one by one, shared the pain of 12 years of insanity caused by his addiction to alcohol. The family group—husband Tom, wife Jean, 18-year-old daughter, 14-year-old son—and an addictions counselor were participating in an intervention session. The meeting was a vital part of the treatment for Tom's alcoholism. He was in an addiction treatment unit and had had two weeks' sobriety.

His wife began to speak. "Tom, I want you to know that we love you and it's hard to do this. But you must get well, or our family will break up. We have all grown apart. I've considered divorce several times. You haven't been a husband or a father for years. I can't understand why we've put up with it so long, except we love you."

It was difficult for Tom to listen, but it was important for him to understand how his drinking had affected each member of his family. Alcohol-free for the first time in years, he could see and feel the pain in his wife's eyes.

Despite the best of intentions, the family behaves in ways that allow the addicted one to continue to use the addicting chemical.[1] Family members protect, make excuses, buy into alibis, and cover up. They might call the employer, claiming the abuser has the flu. Or they might cover a bad check, or retain a lawyer to beat a driving-while-intoxicated charge. Tom's family could plead guilty on all counts.

All of this raises the anxiety level of the family. In turn, the addict uses more alcohol (or whatever he might be addicted to) to reduce his anxiety, and the spiral turns faster. Soon the family can't cope with the addiction any more than the addict can, and the family unit begins to disintegrate.

"What makes me so angry, Dad, is the three years I had to go to a psychiatrist." Peter, Tom's 14-year-old son, confronted his father.

"You had me thinking I was crazy, and all the time it was your drinking. People believed that because I couldn't handle the fighting between you and Mom, I was sick. Well, I see now that I'm not crazy."

Families that face chemical addiction go through several stages of coping behavior as the disease progresses.[2]

Denial—Early in the development of the disease, excessive chemical use is explained away by both marriage partners. Usually tiredness, worry, nervousness, or a bad day is the excuse.

Eliminate the Problem—But when the spouse recognizes that the drinking or drug use is not normal, the abuser is pressed to cut down or quit. So the user tries to cut back or even stop, and at the same time keep up a good front. At this time the children in the family may begin to have behavioral problems in response to the family stress.

Chaos—As the chemical abuse continues, the family structure breaks down—reeling from crisis to crisis. Under unbearable pressure, the spouse is forced to seek outside help.

Reorganization—Reinforced by this help, the nonusing spouse gains strength and brings some structure back into the family. The abusing spouse may also get help and find sobriety.

Efforts to Escape—But if the addicted spouse does not get help, the nonusing spouse often decides to seek separation as a means to survive.

It is important to note that the above outline describes how the family adjustment usually proceeds if the husband is the abuser. But if the wife is the addict, divorce is much more likely to occur early in the process. The wife of a chemically addicted husband, given the economic realities of today's society, is more apt to stay in the marriage because she feels she needs the husband's financial support to maintain the family. On the other hand, men in general are less inclined to seek outside help. Therefore, the husband of an addicted wife may see no other option than divorce to save himself and his family.[3]

Family Reorganization—In the case of separation, family reorganization takes place without the addicted member. But in the happy instance that the using spouse finds sobriety, a reconciliation can take place. However, in either path both parties will have to realign roles in the family and make new adjustments to achieve family recovery.

Recovery—A family systems approach, based on the notion that a change by any member affects the total family, provides the framework for recovery. Several issues must be given priority during this critical time.

While the addict is in treatment, the spouse may be concerned about unpaid bills, child care, loss of trust, broken promises, and so on. Attention must be paid to helping the family deal with the nitty-gritty details of everyday survival. Just as the recovering addict requires a lot of structure and guidance, so does the family.[4] It is vital for the family, including the addict, to be in family counseling with a counselor knowledgeable in chemical addiction. Family members should be involved with Al-Anon or NARANON and the user with Alcoholics or Narcotics Anonymous.

Another issue for the family will be to have realistic expectations for the pace of recovery. Everything is not going to be rosy now that the abuser is in treatment. It's not going to be all bad, either. But things will probably bounce back and forth between the two extremes.

At some point in recovery the family is going to need to share with the user what it was like for them, on an emotional level, to struggle with the disease of addiction. In fact, both the addict and family members must gain some appreciation for what the addiction felt like for the other. This "tell it like it is" cathartic session requires the skill and support of a professional substance-abuse therapist and is best done in a family counseling session. There can be no family closet where secrets or skeletons lurk, for this can interfere with each member's regaining a healthy new life.

Tom and his family were committed to recovery. They worked hard at getting well—they cried together, laughed together, shared their fears and their anger. They are still working at recovery. It hasn't been easy, but they are together.

Endnotes

[1] M. Bowen, "Alcoholism as Viewed Through Family Systems Theory and Family Psychotherapy," *Annals of the New York Academy of Science* 223 (1974): 115-122.

[2] C. Janzen, "Family Treatment for Alcoholism: A Review," *Social Work* 23 (1978): 135-141.

[3] J. Orford, "Alcoholism and Marriage," *Journal of Studies on Alcohol* 36(1978): 1537-1563.

[4] P. Steinglass, "Family Therapy in Alcoholism," in P. Steinglass, ed., *The Biology of Alcoholism* (New York: Plenum Press, 1977), vol. 5.

Adult Children of Addicted Parents

Imagine for a moment what life is like for a child with an addicted parent.

What is it like to lie in bed listening to your parents fight? What is it like when mom often neglects to pack your school lunch? or when you're not allowed to bring friends home to play?

What is it like to be unable to participate in school functions because you must get home to care for your younger brother or sister? or for the money you made mowing lawns to be missing from your room? or . . .

The early homelife of a child of an addicted parent is unpredictable at best—more often than not, it's chaotic. Never certain whether a parent will be sober, drunk, or out of control, these kids have a tough time telling fact from fantasy. They learn to regard chaos as normal and can't readily tell truth from error nor right from wrong. That's because they are frequently raised in homes that lack a consistent role model for adult behavior or healthy relationships. Children of addicted parents have major problems with self-esteem, seldom receiving positive feedback from parents. Because the home environment is so chaotic, the child fails to learn the difference between normal and abnormal behavior.

Individuals who grew up in these chaotic homes bring their troublesome behavior to adult life—to personal and professional associations. The result is a lifetime of disturbed relationships, unless they get professional help.

Warren, a young engineer employed in a high-tech industry, experienced growing difficulty in relating to his fellow workers. He also felt increasingly isolated from his wife and family. Alarmed, he decided to see a counselor.

"Did either of your parents have a drinking problem, Warren?" the therapist asked in the course of getting introductory information.

"My father is an alcoholic, but what difference does that make?" Warren replied, somewhat taken aback by the question.

"You're an adult child of an addicted parent," the counselor explained, "and it could have a great deal to do with the problems you face."

An attractive, well-dressed woman began counseling following a life-shattering divorce. Characterized by pain, conflict, alienation, and bitterness, the marriage of seven years ended when her husband walked out on her to marry a close friend. One question the counselor asked during the first visit puzzled her. "Arlene, does your mother or father have a problem with alcohol or drugs?"

"Why, yes," she answered. "My father has had a problem for as long as I can remember. It caused all kinds of trouble in our home, and he still has a problem."

The reality that chemical addiction is a chronic, progressive, ultimately fatal disease is finally meeting with widespread acceptance. There is also a growing awareness—but not so widespread—that family members need treatment for the disease as much as the addict does. This treatment has focused primarily on the spouse of the user.

Latest research in the field, however, demonstrates that many adults who grew up in families where one or more parents were addicted are at significant risk.[1] Not only do a high percentage of children of addicted parents (up to 80 percent) develop drinking and drug problems, but they also are disturbed in adulthood by emotional turmoil related to living in a chemical dependency home.[2]

Rapidly approaching crisis proportions, 28 million adult children of addicted parents—13 percent of the adult population—are affected by this burgeoning problem.[3]

The counselor's assessment shocked Warren. It never had entered his mind that his difficulties with his family and at work could be the result of his father's abuse of alcohol.

His initial reaction to the counselor's intervention was typical—denial.

"It's hard to believe that my father's drinking affected my life like this."

His counselor had to do some educating before Warren could see the connection.

Arlene also found it difficult to see the relationship.

Both Arlene and Warren, together with most adult children of addicted parents, struggle with six core clinical issues affecting their personality.[4]

Topping the list, and pervading all the others, is the need to be in control. If these people don't have command of their surroundings—family, work, play—they are uneasy. If they lack complete self-control, they get fearful. If they can't be at the helm, in some sense managing others, they feel anxious.

Other issues are: lack of trust, disregard for personal needs, denial of feelings, inability to recognize and set limits, and the tendency to think in mutually exclusive terms—things are all good or all bad, all right or all wrong. These core issues undermine close relationships.

Once they became aware of the way their parents' drinking had shaped their personalities, both Arlene and Warren readily admitted that these issues were significant factors in their problems.

Although professional awareness of the needs of this population is just beginning to develop, the pain and the pathos of the victims have been the subject of song and verse for a century or more. A nineteenth-century classic pictures a young girl in a local bar, pleading with her drunken father to come home and care for the family.

"Father, dear father, come home with me now!
The clock in the steeple strikes one;

You said you were coming right home from the
    shop,
As soon as your day's work was done.
Our fire has gone out, our home is all dark,
And mother's been watching since tea,
With poor brother Benny so sick in her arms,
And no one to help her but me.
Come home! Come home! Come home!
Please, father, dear father, come home."
        —H. C. Work, "Father, Dear Father"

This old favorite, written by the author of
"Grandfather's Clock," touches the heart of the
issue—"no one to help her but *me.*" As youngsters, the children of addicted parents were forced
prematurely into roles of responsibility. As a result, they never learned how to be children, how
to play, how to have a good time. They never
learned how to make friends. These people never
learned the value of truth, for truth has little merit
in an environment of chemical dependency. Personal boundaries are nonexistent in families af-
flicted with the disease of addiction, so these
victims become adults at a time when they really
need to be learning to accept their limits of responsibility, their weaknesses, and their
strengths.

Informed intervention is vital. Unless some outside event compels adult children of addicted
parents to get help, they continue struggling with
life, finding little respite from their pain. They are
vulnerable to becoming addicted themselves. This
intervention could be an informative article on the

topic, a nudge from a concerned friend, or a confrontation by an alert professional.

Once the intervention is made, traditional client-centered therapy, which assumes that the answers reside within the person, is not appropriate. Therapeutic goals should focus on what the adult child missed in adolescence. The counselor should be aware of the issues and know the proper course of treatment for adult children of addicted parents. And one-to-one therapy must be supplemented with educational experiences that help the client learn to play, to set limits, and to establish personal boundaries.

Resources available for these experiences include: Al-Anon, group therapy specifically for adult children of addicted parents, and a variety of workshops dealing with such issues as assertiveness, self-esteem, and values clarification.

The adult child should begin to focus on the following spiritual tools for recovery: easy access to the providence of God; the healing value of community; the rewards of gratitude; and the affirmation that comes from a sense of vocation and personal worth. Using the spiritual tools of recovery influences the adult child to abandon isolation and begin venturing out into the world, where he or she can join hands with the wider community of human beings. The adult child can now begin to take risks and to trust more in self, in others, and in the presence of a Higher Power. Rather than looking backward, life for the adult child becomes prospective, with a new emphasis on the quality of experience.

This growing body of troubled individuals is rapidly becoming the largest group affected by the family disease of addiction. Pastors, therapists, and counselors carrying a regular case load most certainly will encounter adult children of addicted parents. They must become familiar with the treatment issues unique to these people. But until they understand fully the dynamics of addiction and the appropriate treatment for the disease, they should refer these people to Certified Addictions Counselors, Al-Anon, or other special groups for adult children.

Does it make a difference if your parent had a drinking problem? It has had a major impact on your life. If you need help—don't wait, get it.

Endnotes

[1] J. Seixas, "Children From Alcoholic Homes," in *Alcoholism*, N. Estes and M. Heinemann, eds. (St. Louis: C. V. Mosby, 1982).

[2] D. Shah and M. Reese, "Kids of Alcoholics," *Newsweek*, May 28, 1979, p. 82.

[3] J. Kinney and G. Leaton, *Loosening the Grip* (St. Louis: Mosby Company, 1983).

[4] H. Gravits and J. Bowden, "Therapeutic Issues of Adult Children of Alcoholics," *Alcohol Health and Research World*, Summer 1984, pp. 25-36.

Women and Alcohol—Double Trouble

Modern women with a drinking problem are victims of an aggravating paradox. It's called the double standard.

A pretty brunette executive returning from lunch overheard several secretaries talking about her. Joanne was stunned!

"I hate to see her drunk," one observed.

"You're right, she seems to get more aggressive when she's half in the bag," the other responded.

Their scathing criticism stung, but what hurt even more, they made no mention of Don, her fellow executive. He often went to lunch with her and had more difficulty "holding" his liquor than she. Joanne resented being victimized by the double standard, particularly when imposed by women.

Smart, sophisticated, and successful, modern women are increasingly enjoying hard-won equality. But the percentage who use alcohol face a frustrating dilemma. Ironically, the fight for social equality has not secured equality in social drinking.

The dilemma springs from the double standard that has haunted women from ancient times. Today it is still a formidable obstacle in the struggle for women's equality. On the one hand, modern women identify with the Madison Avenue image of the successful career woman who accepts alcohol as a major socializing agent. On the other hand, society still expects women to be guardians of the young and vehicles for passing on the moral values of the race. As a result, more and more women are succumbing to the disease of alcoholism and the stigma of the double standard.

The major responsibility for women's dilemma must be placed on the advertising industry. The media has popularized booze and drugs, pushing pills as the "quick fix" for pain, and alcohol as the cure for loneliness. An attractive male always hovers somewhere in the picture.

Such images have a profound effect on modern women. Studies indicate that 70 percent of all high-school girls and 75 percent of all college women use alcohol.[1] Drinking is no longer considered deviant behavior, as single women are welcomed in bars. Research also shows that women's drinking patterns are determined not by ethnic or family pressures, but by social situations that strongly encourage them to drink.[2, 3]

Kay, married and with a drinking problem, is a victim of the double standard. While throwing a dinner party one memorable evening, she managed to outrage her family. Feeling mellow after a few drinks, she decided to liven up the celebration. Hopping up on a table, she performed a belly dance. Although the guests were amused, her 18-year-old daughter was incensed. Pulling her mother down from the table, she lashed out at Kay, "How could you? Whenever you have a few drinks, you do stupid things!"

As Kay tells it, "This daughter smokes pot and hangs around with a beer-guzzling crowd. When her dad comes home soused and runs the car over the lawn, the flower bed, or the hedge, her comment is 'Oh, that dad, what a crazy nut!' But I get read the riot act. There's no justice!"

The double standard—which holds that "boys will be boys, but women who drink too much betray a sacred trust"—has a vicious sting. Drunken women are whisked out of sight to avoid a spectacle and are shielded from view by those around them. One Alcoholics Anonymous member, the wife of a physician, says, "I was protected almost until I died. No one wanted to notice what was happening to me."

A physician who treats women alcoholics has put it more bluntly: "Men sometimes let their alcoholic wives die rather than embarrass the family by getting help."

Alcoholism is the nation's third-leading cause of death in women between the ages of 35 and 55. Tragically, the conspiracy of silence by family, friends, doctors, hospitals, and law enforcement officials keeps approximately 95 percent of its victims undiagnosed and untreated.[4]

Sadly, coupled with this slow-to-die attitude—which seems to say that a female alcoholic has failed as a woman, wife, and mother—is a woman's own acceptance that she *is* a bum, a lady lush, the stereotyped legacy of the temperance movement.

The frightening results are that women are underrepresented in treatment facilities, get into treatment later and less frequently than males, and are sicker and harder to treat. Winnie Fraser, director of a Canadian detoxification unit, states that women "are usually more deteriorated than men, take longer to detoxify, do not stay as long, and are much less willing to be engaged in further treatment."[5]

Evidence shows that even after the woman alcoholic gains sobriety, she continues to be victimized by the double standard. She will have difficulty reestablishing a normal life and will face gross denial of her rights in employment, welfare, insurance, and child custody.

Centuries-old attitudes have not changed. That's the harsh reality for the woman with a drinking problem. Getting help demands making tough decisions that place her in conflict with friends and family. It demands taking risks just to survive.

Joanne risked alienating her family and entered a hospital for treatment. Now on the road to recovery, she recalls with sadness her husband's disapproval of her going for help.

"I couldn't believe his attitude. He didn't want me to go to the treatment center! It embarrassed him, I suppose. But I needed help."

Alcoholism held her squarely on the horns of the dilemma.

"No matter how he felt," she continued, "I had

to get help. I had no control over my husband's feelings, no control over my drinking. I was powerless over my disease. But I wanted to live."

Modern women addicts have a new assertiveness and independence that they can use to connect with resources and services designed for them.

1. All states and most cities maintain councils on alcoholism, which make appropriate referrals for help.

2. Many treatment centers offer all female treatment programs coordinated by women staff professionals. Women can explore problems without the added burden of living up to a certain image.

3. Alcoholics Anonymous groups for women focus on problems encountered by female alcoholics.

4. Specialized groups for women alcoholics are available at major treatment centers. They include Alternatives to Drinking; Assertiveness Training; Medical, Family, and Psychological Aspects of Female Alcoholism; and others.

Like Joanne, women alcoholics must take a risk to break out of the dilemma of the double standard.

But it's worth it!

Endnotes

[1] J. Rachal et al., *A National Study of Adolescent Drinking Behavior, Attitudes, and Correlates*, prepared for the National Institute on Alcohol Abuse and Alcoholism (Springfield, Va: National Technical Information Service, 1975).

[2] J. S. Tamerin et al., "The Upper-Class Alcoholic: A Syndrome in Itself?" *Psychosomatic Medicine* 12 (1971): 200.

[3] Brown-Mayers et al., *Psychosocial Study of Hospitalized Middle-Class Alcoholic Women in the United States* (White Plains, N.Y.: Bloomingdale Hospital, 1975).

[4] M. Argerion and D. Paulino, "Women Arrested for Drunken Driving in Boston: Social Characteristics and Circumstances of Arrest," *Journal of Studies on Alcohol* 37 (1976): 648.

[5] W. Fraser, "The Alcoholic Woman: Attitudes and Perspectives," in A. MacLennon, ed., *Women: Their Use of Alcohol and Other Legal Drugs*, a provincial consultation (Toronto: Addiction Research Foundation, 1975, 1976).

Additional Reference

Estes, N. J. and M. E. Heinemann. *Alcoholism: Development, Consequences, and Interventions.* Second edition. St. Louis: C. V. Mosby, 1982.

Addiction and Child Sexual Abuse

You could feel the rage and pain as Linda shared her first recollections of a nightmare she'd endured for 11 years.

"I was only 4 years old," she said, "when my father started taking carefully posed nude pictures of me. That's when the abuse began."

The pretty, blonde 27-year-old mother of two was one of seven young women in a support group for sexually abused females. She continued her story.

"It wasn't long before he began touching me where he shouldn't. This progressed to kissing me there and by age 9 to having sex with me. He usually came for me after he had been drinking. Finally when I was 15, I left home. I couldn't stand it any longer."

One out of four women in America is sexually abused before she reaches the age of 18,[1] and one out of seven men suffer the same fate. Sexual exploitation of preschool children in day-care centers across the country has brought this burgeoning problem to public attention.

But the sobering reality is that 75 to 85 percent of abused children know their offenders, and 60 to

70 percent of these offenders are family members who continue that abuse for years.[2]

Alcohol, as Linda suggests, is usually a factor in child sexual abuse. Research shows that 80 percent of the offenders also abuse alcohol. Alcoholism is a stark reality in more than 50 percent of the homes of these victims.[3]

No child is capable emotionally of handling repeated sexual abuse. Even 2- and 3-year-olds, who don't know right from wrong, develop a variety of distressing feelings and thoughts as a result of abuse. In fact, recent research shows that multiple personality problems have their origin in incestuous sexual abuse in early childhood.[4]

Children of 5 or older, knowing and caring for the abuser, become trapped between affection for the person and the sense that the sexual activities are terribly wrong. If such children try to break away from the sexual relationship, the abuser often threatens violence or loss of love. In addition, these children may fear the anger, jealousy, or shame of other family members. They might also be afraid that the family will break up if they tell their sordid secret. Consequently, they learn to keep their pain to themselves.

Prisoners in a silent hell, these kids have no outlet. They don't know how to find relief. Children are not taught to "get out" their feelings. They can't understand the pain and, moreover, no one will listen.

"My mother told me I was imagining things, that I had a vivid fantasy world. My older sister laughed at me, but I found out much later that my father abused her too." Sharon, another member of the therapy group, spoke of the "sacred pact" of silence that exists in these families. No one acknowledges the truth because it is so painful, so out of step with moral and ethical values. It cannot be allowed to surface.

"I realize now that I became a nonperson in order to endure it. I denied myself," Sharon admitted.

Ironically, Sharon finally escaped her silent hell when after eight years of sexual abuse her mother divorced her father—because of his alcoholism!

Barbara, another woman in the group, spoke up. Angrily she spat out her words. "I was abused by gentleness. My father manipulated me with nurturing. He seduced me into sex with affection. It stinks. Years later I learned what an alcoholic con he really was."

Her comments highlight one of the myths about sexual abuse of children. It does *not* usually involve physical force. More often than not, it is accomplished by seduction—with affection, with nurturing, or with fear of the consequences in the family. The alcoholic adult is universally noted for being a skillful con artist.

An unmarried woman in her late 20s shared with the group her memories of feeling sacrificial. June's dad led her to believe that she had an important role in keeping the family together. She was convinced that she could keep her father from drinking.

"I felt so unique," she said. "No one else could do what I was doing. For years I had no idea of the depth of my emotional hell."

When that awareness hit, however, she became severely depressed and suicidal. June has drifted in and out of therapy for more than 10 years.

"I couldn't fit in with other teenage girls at school," she went on. "They would talk, with questioning innocence, about their maturing sexuality, and I realized I knew it all. I had done it all. My father robbed me of my childhood. He didn't need me—he used me. Besides, he never did stop drinking."

June's agony brings up another myth. Sexual abuse of children, particularly incest, is not misplaced affection. On the contrary, it is misuse of power by the offender.[5] It is spawned by feelings of inadequacy, powerlessness, and insecurity. Most offenders are themselves children of addicted parents and were abused when they were young. Struggling with poor self-esteem throughout their lives, they find devious ways to feel powerful.

Children victimized by prolonged sexual abuse usually develop low self-esteem, feelings of worthlessness, and a distorted sexuality. These kids may become withdrawn and mistrustful of adults. They could become suicidal.

Some children have difficulty relating to others except on sexual terms. Many grow up to be child abusers themselves or develop other serious emotional problems; they quite likely will become substance abusers.

Consistent information from addiction treatment centers shows that one of every two women admitted for treatment has been sexually abused as a child by family members.[6] These patients are usually adult children of alcoholic parents.

Sexual abuse of children has grown far beyond our awareness of the problem. It has reached the point where at least 25 percent of the nation's female children are victims. And every one of them feels powerless to break out of this silent hell. Not only that, the ordeal has the potential of permanently distorting their lives.

Fortunately, because of groups such as the one Linda and her friends have joined, information is emerging that can help victims find relief.

It is vital that friends, family members, and professional care-givers alike be sensitive to symptoms, both in children and in their families, that point to child sexual abuse. Often one can find no physical signs of child abuse, or only a physician can detect the signs. So it is important to be aware that the behavior of sexually abused children may include the following:[7, 8, 9]

- Excessive sexual play
- Unusual interest or avoidance of things of a sexual nature
- Masturbation
- Bed-wetting
- Early depression
- Suicidal ideas
- Isolation
- Sleep problems, nightmares
- Refusal to go to school, or delinquency
- Unusual aggressiveness

Topping the list of family symptoms is alcoholism. Also, the family is often characterized by secrecy, splitting up, depression, detachment, low self-esteem, and certain members living a double life. Sensitivity to the meaning of these symptoms can lead to early treatment for the abused and the family. But this requires the willingness to confront the problem, which also means confronting the offender. For obvious reasons, child molesters do not seek help on their own. Ninety percent of the child abusers presently in treatment are there because of court order.

Child abusers suffer from a deep-seated illness, and treatment is lengthy, up to three years. It must be accomplished outside the home and in a group setting where the offender learns how to manage this chronic, lifelong disease.

There *is,* however, hope—hope for the abused child, for the family, and for the offender. But more effective ways to make help readily accessible need to be found. Fortunately, a number of resources are beginning to be developed, but more must be made available, particularly to the kids.

Sharon put it this way: "We didn't have telephone hotlines when I was a kid. Boy, I would have welcomed one that said, 'If your father bothers you, call this number.'"

Endnotes

[1] D. Russell, "The Incidence and Prevalence of Intrafamilial and Extrafamilial Sexual Abuse of Females," *Child Abuse and Neglect* 7 (1983).

[2] P. V. DiVasto et al., "The Prevalence of Sexually Stressful

Events Among Females in the General Population," *Archives of Sexual Behavior* 13, No. 1 (1984).

[3] F. S. Cohen and J. Densen-Gerber, "A Study of the Relationship Between Child Abuse and Drug Addiction in 178 Patients—Preliminary Report," *Child Abuse and Neglect* 6 (1982): 383-387.

[4] E. S. Bowman et al., "Multiple Personality in Adolescence: Relationship to Incestual Experience," *Journal of the American Academy of Child Psychiatry* 24, No. 1 (1985): 109-114.

[5] M. de Chesnay, "Father-Daughter Incest," *Journal of Psychosocial Nursing* 22, No. 9 (September 1984).

[6] J. Benward and J. Densen-Gerber, "Incest as a Causative Factor in Antisocial Behavior: An Exploratory Study," *Contemporary Drug Problems* 4 (1975): 322-340.

[7] De Chesnay.

[8] "Child Sexual Abuse—Some Facts on a Shocking Problem," *EAP Digest*, July/August 1985, pp. 67, 68.

[9] T. M. Anglin, "Physician Management of Sexually Abused Children and Adolescents," *Current Problems in Pediatrics* 14, No. 7 (July 1984).

We're Not Helpless

In the face of the overwhelming evidence of widespread use and abuse of alcohol and drugs, it would seem that the rest of the population, the nonusers, can only sit back and be victimized by this disease. But such is not the case.

Surprisingly, most people, users and nonusers alike, lack awareness of this rapidly growing threat to society. Misconceptions about the effects of alcohol and drugs, and the outright denial of the danger, encourage broad public apathy.

Commenting on this perplexing attitude, the director of public safety of a large metropolitan county said, "Somehow I think it was believed that if the problem were ignored, it would go away."* But it won't go away until we get provoked enough to take action. The resources and energies of a broad spectrum of concerned individuals and organizations—courts, police, nurses, physicians, clergy, churches, social workers, parents, and business leaders—are needed to combat this burgeoning problem.

Three areas clamor for swift action.

1. Drug Education—Up-to-the-minute, authoritative, unslanted drug education for youngsters and young adults ages 12-35 is needed now to counteract the false information surrounding the abuse of alcohol and drugs.

Parent-Teacher Associations could take the initiative and use their power to press for objective and effective drug education. They can pressure their school systems to ask experts in substance abuse to provide in-service education for teachers. Parent-teacher groups can demand that substance-abuse information be integrated into as many subject areas as possible. They can also help students assume leadership roles in educating their peers in the perils of drug abuse.

Teenagers are not unique in their distorted ideas about the effects of alcohol and drugs. These garbled notions permeate the thinking of the 25- to 35-year-old group as well. Young adult middle-class America of the eighties is the Woodstock generation of the sixties and seventies. Drinking is not only chic; it is virtually mandatory. So is pot smoking. The New York *Times,* December 11, 1983, reported that smoking pot is so fashionable that it is "currently our second-largest cash crop nationally, after corn."

No church or synagogue is immune to this problem. A good share of these misinformed young people are active and respected members of religious communities across the United States. No church member or clergyperson can avoid their responsibility to address this threat.

Drug education in the parish is a logical place to start. Led by clergy, the religious community must own up to its role in this nationwide problem. We have learned to handle our pressure, loneliness, frustration, and aging with legally prescribed psychoactive drugs and alcohol. It is no wonder many of our youngsters and young contemporaries turn to drugs so easily.

Parish lay leaders, together with clergy, can integrate substance-abuse information into present educational programs for the congregation.

Health professionals also need reliable drug education. Traditionally medicine, psychiatry, and the social services have mistakenly believed drug dependence to be a symptom of a deeply rooted neurosis that must be treated first if the addiction is to be eliminated. Mounting evidence demonstrates that addiction is a separate disease, an illness that devastates the physical, psychological, and spiritual dimensions of life. The addict can only be successfully treated in a program that includes detoxification combined with education and individual and group therapy.

The helping professions, of course, can make a substantial contribution in the fight to combat the drug menace. But first they must understand the true nature of the problem. Reliable, state-of-the-art seminars, lectures, and courses that address substance abuse are offered regularly in strategic places across the country. Information about these educational opportunities can be obtained from regional and state drug abuse agencies. Designed specifically for the health professional, they usually offer continuing education credits required to maintain licensure.

Also, concerned physicians and medical societies should press medical schools to add substance-abuse courses to their curricula. Physicians today graduate from medical school with only a smattering of information concerning the nation's fourth-leading killer disease—chemical addiction.

2. Public Policy—Our collective efforts are needed in the field of public policy. Legislation regulating drug abuse is largely hodgepodge, makes little common sense, and is years behind the real world. Laws governing the use of alcohol and pot together are practically nonexistent. Some states mandate Breathalyzer tests to determine the blood-alcohol content of motorists suspected of driving under the influence. But only a handful have similar laws requiring blood or urine tests of drivers who might be under the influence of marijuana.

Guidelines that establish intoxication levels similar to alcohol are needed for marijuana. This would help in developing legislation to regulate the use of alcohol and pot among drivers of motor vehicles.

As individuals and members of civic-minded groups, we can lobby our legislators to produce laws that will provide adequate protection for the unsuspecting public and begin to bring this menace under control.

We can also work with the local bar associations, pressing for legislation directed at drug impairment. The sight-impaired are restricted from driving automobiles, flying aircraft, etc. Why not have similar restrictions imposed on the drug-impaired? Jobs that affect public safety—airline pilots and mechanics, train operators, bus drivers, law enforcement officers, school bus drivers, nuclear reactor personnel, and others—should require drug-free status. We, the innocent public, deserve this protection.

3. Personal Responsibility—Those who are closest to the primary victims of this disease—the abusers caught in the web of addiction—have a responsibility to recognize the earliest symptoms of chemical addiction displayed by friends, family members, and professional associates. Not only do we need to be able to recognize these symptoms; we must act and confront the issue. If we chose not to confront the user, we then become part of the problem. We become enablers, participating in the denial of the reality of the disease and thus helping the user to continue on a self-destructive path. This course can lead only to disaster.

We are not helpless in the battle against drug abuse. On the contrary, there is much each of us can do. This is not a struggle in which we have the luxury of sitting on the sidelines and watching. Only two choices confront us: we can join the side that actively struggles to defeat drug abuse, or we can sit on the side that enables it to thrive.

Which way do you choose?

Endnote

* Personal interview with J. Danzilli, June 1, 1979.

Drug Addiction—A Challenge for the Religious Community

No church is immune to the effects of the raging epidemic of drug addiction. We might like to think so, but we would be mistaken. The ravages of this disease know no boundaries, not even religious ones.

Sadly, it appears that a good share of the nation's religious community is not prepared to help the victims of addiction find healing. Perhaps we prefer that alcoholics remain anonymous.

The facts are that one out of every two Americans is either addicted to alcohol or drugs, or else their life is adversely affected by someone close who is hooked on some chemical.

And whether we believe it or not, the symptoms and pathology of this epidemic reach, tentacle-like, into every church and synagogue in the nation. Its victims fall all about us.

Unfortunately, the community of faith has not been an effective healer in this field. This is the regrettable paradox: what the church purports to give freely—spiritual healing—it seems unable to offer to the victims of addiction in its midst. But the church or synagogue has more to offer than any other organization, both in preventing addiction and aiding in recovery.

Several factors make the spiritual community a potentially effective source of healing for substance abusers. First, parish leaders have easy access to homes. No other group of professional care-givers enjoys such a close relationship with individuals and families. Second, pastors, priests, and rabbis are approachable. Research has consistently shown that the majority of people needing help turn first to a clergy person. Third, spiritual leaders are viewed as family educators and exemplars. And fourth, religious leaders speak regularly on issues of social and moral responsibility.

These four elements form the basis of a positive therapeutic partnership that we can use to fight addiction. But church leaders will need more than just a partnership if they are to be really helpful. They also need education and compassion.

In light of the seriousness of the drug-abuse problem, it seems strange that many religious leaders graduate from the seminary without having had any instruction in dealing with chemical dependency. Also, precious little education in drug dependency takes place in our churches and synagogues.

The first step in becoming an effective healer is to understand that addiction is a killer disease. It devastates the total being—physical, psychological, and spiritual. But the primary site of this disorder is in the human spirit. All the rest— shakes, weeping, horrors, vomiting, hallucinations, delirium tremens—are physical and psychological reactions to an underlying spiritual illness.

Chemical addiction jeopardizes the victim's link with God, smothers faith, demolishes self-esteem, undermines moral values, and closes the heart's door to grace. If left untreated, it cripples and eventually destroys the basic elements of spiritual life. Unfortunately, only 35 to 40 percent of sufferers ever experience recovery.[1]

The next step is to accept the chemical abuser as a helpless victim, not a hopeless sinner. Compassion dictates that we treat these unfortunates as people who can be helped, not as criminals who must be put out of fellowship—out of sight, out of mind.

Understanding the relationships that develop within the family of the substance abuser is also important. Addiction is a social disorder, a family disease in which roles play a significant part. The main role, of course, is that of the *user*—the dependent, isolated denier who needs to use chemicals. Then there is the *victim*—the person who assumes responsibility for and does the addict's work. By so doing, the victim protects the user from the consequences of the disease. The *provoked one* is the family member who acts out anger in various ways, attempting to coerce the addicted person to quit; but this only adds to the user's guilt. The *enabler* plays the key role in the family system, unconsciously perpetuating the user's substance abuse and continued denial of the problem. The enabler is the guilt-ridden "Mr. Clean," who assumes the role of savior.

91

Typically, the spouse of the abuser gets caught up in the role of enabler. In an attempt to keep peace or preserve the marriage relationship, the enabler covers up problems: calling in sick when the user can't make it to work, making excuses to the children when a drinking parent's behavior is questionable, turning the other cheek when the using spouse becomes abusive. This enabling behavior becomes part of the denial system and encourages the addicted one to continue abusing chemicals. Avoiding direct confrontation does not help; it perpetuates the problem.

Well-meaning pastors and church and synagogue members often forfeit their opportunity to be healers by assuming the role of savior and so become enablers. By attempting to reduce the tension and pain in a family victimized by addiction, members of the religious community often join hands with the enabling spouse and in effect become part of the problem. The appropriate helping role in the recovery process is to lead the addict and family into a treatment program and help them stay there.

It is vital for members of the congregation to recognize addiction for what it is—a treatable disease. Focusing on the recovery and growth of the spirit, treatment moves the abuser: (1) from an "I'm the boss" attitude to an awareness of God as the source of help; (2) from "I don't need help" to reaching out to the Source of help; (3) from "There is nothing wrong with me" to confession: "I'm an alcoholic"; (4) from "I'll do it my way" to an act of faith: "I'll do it Your way"; (5) from "I'm unforgivable" to grace, making amends and restoration: "Please forgive me"; (6) from the loneliness of "I don't need anyone" to the security of a healing community: "I can't do it alone"; (7) from the hopelessness of "I am worthless" to a sense of personal value: "I want to share with you what I have been given."

Recovery rises, phoenix-like, out of intense suffering. It comes in response to treatment that fosters honesty, true values, and responsibility. The substance abuser learns through moral and spiritual education that faithful and unselfish work, reverence for family and others, selfless love, obedience to truth and to one's Higher Power, produce a rewarding life. Spiritual conversion plus abstinence equals recovery. This treatment works. Statistics show that 65 to 75 percent of addicts who want to recover do get well when they follow this treatment plan.[2]

Getting an addicted member of the local congregation involved in treatment may require confronting the family with the reality of the disease by intervening in the denial system. This will inevitably increase family anxiety and tension. Therefore, the pastor or church member doing the confronting must be prepared to be an agent of pain in order to bring about recovery to the addicted member and family.

From a theological perspective, we must forgo the urge to be the good Samaritan and instead be the father of the prodigal. The father avoided being the enabler and, painful though it was, permitted his son to suffer the consequences of his actions. Ultimately this detachment permitted the son to come to himself and return home. Offering dignity, love, and acceptance, the father warmly restored his son to the family.

In our churches and synagogues countless prodigals—victims of this menacing epidemic—silently struggle alone, searching for release, for understanding, for acceptance. They are powerless and need help. As church members, we are in a unique and coveted position. We can direct our hurting friends to expert professional and volunteer resources. We can educate and motivate our churches and synagogues to become healing communities that give affirmation and support to these prodigals. We can offer dignity and restoration.

In order to bring relief to these people, the spiritual healers themselves must have help. We must be willing to join hands with other concerned care-givers—physicians and nurses for physical needs, psychiatrists and social workers for psychological and social needs—to offer effective treatment.

There are organizations equipped to aid in helping substance abusers find sobriety. These groups offer excellent resources for the religious organization. For example, for alcohol abuse they include Alcoholics Anonymous for the abuser, Al-Anon for the family, Alateen for the children, and local referral centers for professional treatment.

We, individual members and religious congregations alike, cannot afford to continue to deny the reality of this raging epidemic. It threatens all of us. The challenge for us is to mobilize our resources and help those in our midst who, without our help, might die of this life-threatening illness.

Endnotes

[1] N. J. Estes and M. E. Heinemann, *Alcoholism* (St. Louis: C. V. Mosby, 1982).

[2] "Current Drug Use, March 30, 1984, National Household Survey," *NIDA Capsule*, March 1984.